6/1/16

Creepy Libraries

by Troy Taylor

Consultant: Paul F. Johnston, PhD
Washington, DC

BEARPORT
PUBLISHING

New York, New York

Credits

Cover and Title Page, © Kim Jones; 6, © Kate Sherrill; 7T, © Courtesy of Willard Library of Evansville; 7B, © Courtesy of Willard Library of Evansville; 8, © Michael Weaver; 9T, © Photo Courtesy of Donna Albino, http://www.mtholyoke.edu/~dalbino; 9M, © avarand/Shutterstock; 9B, © villax/Shutterstock; 10T, © NRT/Shutterstock; 10B, © Daniel Westfall; 11T, © Eric Isselee/Shutterstock; 11L, © Africa Studio/Shutterstock; 11R, © Mike Tewkesbury; 12, © Loucindy Weitzman; 13T, © Lahutkin Anatolii/Shutterstock; 13B, © OJO_Images/iStock; 14, © Emily Han; 15T, © Special Collections, Library, Arts & Culture Dept., Glendale, CA; 15B, © Jeremy Sternberg; 16, © Brigida Blasi; 17T, © isoga/Shutterstock; 17B, © Federico Rostagno/Shutterstock; 18, © Frank C. Grace; 19, © From the Collection of the Millicent Library; 20, © Michael Lynch; 21T, © Billings Public Library; 21B, © Flair Images/iStock; 22, © Sherpes; 23T, © Lario Tus/Shutterstock; 23B, © shalunishka/Shutterstock; 24, © Jenny Antill Clifton; 25T, © Jess Zimbabwe; 25BL, © GlobalP/iStock; 25BR, © PrinceOfLove/Shutterstock; 26, © B.M. Hoppe/CC-BY-SA-3.0; 27T, © Oleg Kozlov/Shutterstock; 27BL, © Olga Nikonova/Shutterstock; 27BR, © Nadya Lukic/Shutterstock; 31, © Jjustas/Shutterstock.

Publisher: Kenn Goin
Editor: Jessica Rudolph
Creative Director: Spencer Brinker
Design: Dawn Beard Creative
Cover: Kim Jones
Photo Researcher: Picture Perfect Professionals, LLC

Library of Congress Cataloging-in-Publication Data

Taylor, Troy, author.
 Creepy libraries / by Troy Taylor.
    pages cm. — (Scary places)
 Includes bibliographical references and index.
 ISBN 978-1-62724-862-4 (library binding) — ISBN 1-62724-862-5 (library binding)
 1. Haunted places—Juvenile literature. 2. Libraries—Juvenile literature. 3. Ghosts—Juvenile literature. I. Title. II. Series: Scary places.
 BF1461.T383 2015
 133.1'22—dc23
                                      2015015234

For more information, write to Bearport Publishing Company, Inc., 45 West 21st Street, Suite 3B, New York, New York 10010. Printed in the United States of America.

10 9 8 7 6 5 4 3 2

Contents

Libraries can be creepy places. They have silent rooms and long, dusty passageways with towering shelves. They are filled with dark shadows and quiet footsteps. You never know when someone might be lurking around a corner or watching you. Now imagine a library that's also filled with ghosts!

In this book you will visit 11 of the spookiest libraries in the United States and meet the terrifying **spirits** who haunt them. Among the spirits are a girl whose image is forever captured in a beautiful **stained-glass window**, a school principal who still watches over her students despite being dead, and a night watchman who died long ago but still plays his violin.

The Grey Lady

Willard Library, Evansville, Indiana

Willard Carpenter was a wealthy man who lived in Evansville in the 1800s. When he died in 1883, he left much of his fortune to the town so that a huge library could be built. This angered his daughter, Louise, who wanted the fortune for herself. In 1908, Louise died—and reportedly came back from the dead to haunt the Willard Library. Today, her ghost is known as the Grey Lady.

The Willard Library

A **custodian** first saw Louise's ghost in the library in 1937. While working in the basement, he spotted the figure of a woman in a long grey dress, grey shawl, and grey veil. The custodian was so scared he dropped the flashlight he was holding. The flashlight flickered off, and when he turned it back on, the woman had vanished!

Louise Carpenter

Since then, many other staff members have spotted the Grey Lady. One librarian said that while construction work was being done in the building, the ghost followed her home! After the construction was finished, the Grey Lady came back to the library—and has been there ever since.

Because so many people around the country are interested in the Grey Lady, the library has installed **ghost cams**. Now everyone can watch for the ghost on the Internet.

This picture shows a view of the library from one of the ghost cams. Could this be the Grey Lady?

Still at School

Reid Memorial Library, Godfrey, Illinois

Some people are so passionate about what they do that they show up to their workplaces even if they are sick. However, a schoolteacher and principal named Harriet Haskell showed up to work even after she had died! Today, her ghost remains at the school where she spent much of her life.

The Reid Memorial Library

In 1867, Harriet became the principal of a girls' college in Illinois called the Monticello **Seminary**. Harriet was beloved by her students. When she died in 1907, former students from all over the country came back to Illinois for her funeral.

Harriet Haskell

Many years later, in 1971, the Monticello Seminary became Lewis and Clark Community College. The previous school's **chapel**—Harriet's favorite room—was turned into a library. It is said that Harriet's spirit lives on in this room. Security guards claim they hear the elevator run at night when nobody else is in the building. Sometimes lights turn on and off and water faucets run for no reason. Some librarians have even seen Harriet's ghost! The ghost is dressed in clothes much like the ones Harriet would have worn in the 1800s.

Why did Harriet's spirit start appearing in the library? No one knows for sure. Although the events are spooky, everyone is happy that Harriet is still around. They feel like she's watching over the school she loved.

Lilacs

Some people say they can smell **lilacs** in the library when no one else is around. This is the scent of a perfume Harriet wore when she was alive.

A Collection of Ghosts

Carnegie Library, Parkersburg, West Virginia

An abandoned library in West Virginia spent years collecting dust before a bookstore moved into the space. Today, the building provides a wonderful home for books—and many ghosts.

The Carnegie Library
in Parkersburg

In 1904, wealthy businessman Andrew Carnegie **donated** thousands of dollars to the town of Parkersburg in West Virginia to build a library. The library closed in 1976 and sat empty until 1985, when it was turned into the Trans-Allegheny Bookstore.

Today, the building is the largest used bookstore in West Virginia—and possibly the most haunted. Several different ghosts are said to be living there, including three women, a well-dressed man, a little girl, and three cats. Some people have claimed that they tripped over a cat on the circular iron staircase, only to turn back and find nothing there.

Visitors have seen other signs of hauntings. Books fly off the shelves, overhead lamps sway back and forth, and lights flicker on and off. The former library is a great place to buy books, but some customers leave quickly after finding ghosts instead!

One of the bookstore's ghosts is believed to be a newspaper reporter who was murdered in her home in 1989. She had spent much of her time digging for facts at the old Carnegie Library. It seems that after her death, she decided to return to the building she knew so well.

Inside the library

A Playful Ghost

Bridgeport Public Library, Bridgeport, Connecticut

About 40 years after the Bridgeport Public Library opened in 1881, a new library was built where the old one stood—and a ghost moved right into the new building. Staff members describe her as a helpful spirit who puts books back on the shelves. However, she is also known as a prankster.

The Bridgeport Public Library

Late one night in February 2006, the **library director** was called at his home because the library's alarm had gone off. Thinking someone might have broken into the building, he rushed there. When he got to the library, he saw that all the lights on the fifth floor were on and a door that had been closed was open. He turned off the lights, closed the door, and went back home.

About an hour after he left, the alarm went off again. This time, several police officers came to search the library. When they looked around the building, they saw that the lights had been turned on again and the door was open. The officers also thought they heard the sound of someone flipping the pages of a book—but there was nobody else in the building. Was it the library's ghost causing some late-night **mischief**?

Although library workers don't know what their ghostly helper was called when she was alive, they have named her Lola.

An Eerie Voice

Brand Library, Glendale, California

In 1904, Leslie Coombs Brand built a beautiful white mansion. Brand died in 1925 and donated his home to the town of Glendale, California, so it could be used as a library. Some people believe that he returned to the library after his death.

The Brand Library

Many staff members say Brand's spirit sometimes speaks in a low voice or makes sudden, unsettling appearances. One day, librarian Joseph Fuchs saw a man walk up a set of stairs not open to the public. Before Joseph had a chance to say something, the man disappeared. Joseph couldn't believe his eyes. Another time, Joseph was working alone in the library at night when he heard a low, moaning voice say, "Joe." Scared out of his wits, Joseph quickly ran out of the building.

Leslie Coombs Brand

The strange sounds and eerie visions have affected other library workers, too. The library's custodians refuse to work alone at night. They're afraid they might see the ghost of Leslie Coombs Brand—the man who refuses to leave his former home.

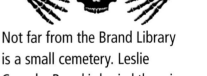

Not far from the Brand Library is a small cemetery. Leslie Coombs Brand is buried there in a **mausoleum** shaped like a pyramid.

15

Can't Rest in Peace

Sweetwater County Library, Green River, Wyoming

For years, people who work at the Sweetwater County Library have reported ghostly sights and sounds. Could that be because the library was built on top of an old graveyard?

The Sweetwater County Library

In 1926, the dead bodies and headstones in the Green River cemetery were dug up and moved so houses could be built on the land. Years later, in 1978, a new library was also built there. However, as construction on the library started, workers began to find skeletons and coffins. It seems some of the bodies that were supposed to have been moved decades earlier were still in the ground.

The library's staff believes the **phantoms** of the people whose graves were disturbed now haunt the library. Workers have reported seeing **typewriters** type by themselves and feeling as though someone is watching them. One maintenance worker saw a vacuum cleaner operate on its own and curtains open and close by themselves. Another library worker reported seeing weird, glowing lights and hearing eerie music.

The creepy sights and sounds became so constant—and scared so many staff members—that the library director eventually rearranged the schedule so nobody had to work at night. With no employees around at night, will the ghosts finally get some peace?

A mummy

In 1985, the **foundation** of the library began to sink into the ground, so repairs had to be made. While workers were digging, they found a small coffin with the body of a child inside. The boy was almost perfectly preserved, much like a **mummy**.

The Girl in the Window

Millicent Library, Fairhaven, Massachusetts

The colorful stained-glass window in a library in Massachusetts shows a beautiful young woman whose life was cut short. Could she be haunting the place that was built as a **memorial** to her?

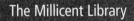
The Millicent Library

In 1890, Henry Huttleston Rogers built a magnificent library and named it after his daughter, Millicent, who died when she was just 17 years old. The library has a huge stained-glass window that includes a portrait of Millicent. The girl remains in the library in another way, though—as a ghost. **Patrons** claim to have heard Millicent laughing and seen her dancing in the aisles between the bookshelves.

Yet is Millicent the only ghost in the library? Some people say they have also seen a woman dressed in black running her fingers along the bookshelves. As soon as she is spotted, she vanishes.

Could some of Millicent's dead family members also be staying in the building? In one room of the library hang several paintings of members of the Rogers family. **Cold spots** are often reported near the pictures. Also, some say that if a person speaks directly to the portraits, the faces in the pictures will react to what is being said!

When Millicent was alive, she loved reading poetry. In the center of the library's stained-glass window, Millicent is shown as the Muse of Poetry. According to Greek **legends**, muses inspired writers and artists in their work. It is said that the girl in the window inspired many great writers, including Mark Twain, whose books can be found on the library's shelves.

The stained-glass window showing Millicent (center)

Spirits on the Move

Parmly Billings Library, Billings, Montana

The Parmly Billings Library was named in honor of the son of Frederick Billings, the town's **founder**. Billings's son, Parmly, died suddenly when he was only 25 years old. Over the years, the library moved to different buildings. During this time, various ghosts have been reported in the different locations—including spirits that have apparently moved along with the books!

The original Billings Library

The original Parmly Billings Library was built in 1901. By 1969, the growing community needed a larger library, so town leaders chose a large red brick building as the new location. It is said that the original castle-like building was haunted. It is also said that when the books and furniture from the old library were moved to the new one, the ghosts moved, too.

The second Billings Library

Staff members and visitors have seen a number of spirits in the red brick library, including a girl in a frilly dress and a man wearing a jean jacket. One library employee saw a very tall spirit that was the color of smoke. Just after it was seen, the spirit disappeared into thin air.

Who are these ghosts? Could they be staff members or former library patrons who died long ago? No one knows, but the spirits seem content to be in the Billings Library—no matter where it's located.

In 2014, the Billings Library moved again. The staff brought along all the old books and furniture from the previous library—and soon after, ghosts were being reported in the new building!

A Ghost at Home

Andrew Bayne Memorial Library, Pittsburgh, Pennsylvania

In 1912, Amanda Bayne Balph passed away, and her house in Pennsylvania was turned into a library. The library included all the books Amanda once owned. She may have loved her books and home so much that she never left them—even long after her death.

The Andrew Bayne Memorial Library

Andrew Bayne was a wealthy farmer who gave his daughter, Amanda, a plot of land to build a house. She and her husband built a brick house and filled it with books. Amanda loved to read. She also loved to look out the house's large windows at the elm trees outside. After Amanda and her husband died, their house was turned into the town's library.

Amanda's books stayed with the library—and it seems she did, too. Many librarians and patrons have reported hearing mysterious footsteps and seeing lights flash on. One day during children's story time, an overhead fan started spinning by itself. Staff members saw this as a sign that Amanda, who never had children, enjoyed having kids in her former home.

Many visitors have also reported seeing a woman looking out the second-story window—the bedroom where Amanda died. How do they know it was Amanda's ghost? The spirit looks just like the photograph of Amanda that hangs above the library's fireplace.

Amanda's favorite elm tree outside her home was named the "Lone **Sentinel**" and was at least 200 years old when she died. In the 1990s, the tree was cut down. After this happened, Amanda's ghost became more active in the library.

Music from Beyond

Julia Ideson Library, Houston, Texas

Located in downtown Houston is the Julia Ideson Library, an old three-story building with many mysteries. One of the mysteries involves two resident ghosts—a former library worker who died in the building in 1936, and his loyal dog. Are the ghosts refusing to leave the library they lived in decades ago?

The Julia Ideson Library

Long ago, the Julia Ideson Library was home to Jacob Frank Cramer, an elderly man who worked as a night watchman, gardener, and handyman for the library. Jacob and his German shepherd, Petey, lived in the library's basement. At night, when the library was closed, he and the dog would climb the stairs to the top floor. Then Jacob would play his violin, filling the building with music.

Inside the library

Today, years after their deaths, Jacob and Petey may still live in the library. Visitors and staff claim to have heard the click-click-click of a dog's nails tapping on the tile floors. When they look for the source of the sound, there is no dog to be found. Others say that **sheet music**, normally kept in a locked room, is sometimes found scattered around the library.

Creepiest of all, however, is when people hear faint violin music playing throughout the library. Could it be Jacob, returning to fill the building with the beautiful music he made when he was alive?

The sound of eerie violin music is usually heard in the library on days when the weather is gloomy.

25

So Many Ghosts!

Blanche Skiff Ross Memorial Library, Nevada, Missouri

The Blanche Skiff Ross Memorial Library, located on the **campus** of Cottey College in Missouri, has a long, strange history. Built on the site of a former hospital, the library is said to be haunted by the ghosts of people who died **gruesome** deaths.

The Blanche Skiff Ross Memorial Library

There are a lot of ghostly tales about Cottey College. Many stories involve the college's library, which was built in 1963 on the site where a hospital once stood. Some students and library staff say they have seen several eerie spirits. One of them is Madame Blitz, the college's former music teacher. In 1904, she killed herself by drinking acid, and she may still haunt the school today. People say they can hear the old teacher playing music in the library.

The most famous ghost is Vera Neitzert, who was a student at Cottey in the 1920s. She was cooking one night when her nightgown caught fire. Vera was seriously burned and died soon after in the hospital that was located where the library now stands. Today her ghost wanders up and down the halls, knocking over stacks of books. Some claim to smell a burning odor just before her ghost is seen.

In the 1860s, there was a terrible fire in the town of Nevada, Missouri. Many people who were injured in the fire later died in the hospital where the Blanche Skiff Ross Memorial Library now stands. Are some of the library's ghosts people who were killed by the fire? Nobody knows for sure.

Creepy Libraries

Parmly Billings Library
Billings, Montana

As this library has moved to different locations, so have its ghosts.

Sweetwater County Library
Green River, Wyoming

This library was built on top of an old cemetery, disturbing the graveyard's occupants.

Reid Memorial Library
Godfrey, Illinois

A dead principal still watches over students in a college library.

Willard Library
Evansville, Indiana

The Grey Lady, still angry that her father didn't leave his fortune to her, haunts this library.

Brand Library
Glendale, California

The man who built a mansion that was turned into a library refuses to leave—even after death.

Julia Ideson Library
Houston, Texas

A musical handyman and his dog haunt this beautiful building.

Blanche Skiff Ross Memorial Library
Nevada, Missouri

This library is haunted by several ghosts, including a woman who killed herself by drinking acid.

Carnegie Library
Parkersburg, West Virginia

This old library, later turned into a bookstore, has been home to a number of ghosts, including a newspaper reporter who was murdered.

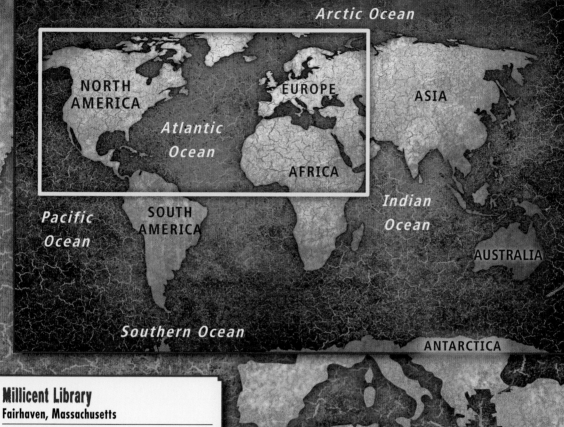

Arctic Ocean

NORTH AMERICA

EUROPE

ASIA

Atlantic Ocean

AFRICA

Indian Ocean

Pacific Ocean

SOUTH AMERICA

AUSTRALIA

Southern Ocean

ANTARCTICA

Millicent Library
Fairhaven, Massachusetts

A long-dead young girl still walks among her beloved books.

Bridgeport Public Library
Bridgeport, Connecticut

A helpful ghost named Lola puts books back on shelves, but she is also known to play pranks.

Andrew Bayne Memorial Library
Pittsburgh, Pennsylvania

A woman who died in a house that became a library leaves many clues that she'll never leaver her home.

Glossary

campus (KAM-puhss) the land and building or buildings that make up a school

chapel (CHAP-uhl) a building or room used for praying

cold spots (KOHLD SPOTS) a small area where the air feels colder than the air around it, thought by some to be caused by the presence of ghosts

custodian (kuh-STOH-dee-uhn) a person who cleans and takes care of a building

donated (DOH-nayt-id) gave as a gift

foundation (foun-DAY-shuhn) a base made of stone, concrete, or other material that supports a building from underneath

founder (FOUN-dur) a person who establishes a town or city

ghost cams (GOHST KAMZ) cameras set up to record paranormal activity such as the movements of a ghost

gruesome (GROO-suhm) horrible; causing horror or disgust

legends (LEJ-uhnds) stories that are handed down from the past that may be based on fact but are not always completely true

library director (LYE-brehr-ee duh-REK-tur) a person in charge of managing a library's staff

lilacs (LYE-laks) a plant with sweet-smelling pink, purple, or white flowers

mausoleum (maw-zuh-LEE-uhm) a large tomb that sits aboveground, where a dead body is housed

memorial (muh-MOR-ee-uhl) something that is built to remember a person who has died

mischief (MISS-chif) playful behavior that may cause trouble

mummy (MUH-mee) the preserved body of a dead person

patrons (PAY-truhnz) people who use the services offered by a business

phantoms (FAN-tuhmz) ghosts or spirits

seminary (SEM-uh-nehr-ee) a school at or above the high school level

sentinel (SEN-ti-nuhl) a soldier who guards an entrance

sheet music (SHEET MYOO-zik) musical notes printed on sheets of paper

spirits (SPIHR-its) supernatural beings, such as ghosts

stained-glass window (STAYND-glass WIN-doh) a window made of colored glass

typewriters (TYPE-*rye*-turz) machines that print letters or numbers onto sheets of paper when the keys are pressed

Bibliography

Leslie, Mark. *Tomes of Terror: Haunted Bookstores and Libraries.* Toronto, Ontario, Canada: Dundurn (2014).

Marimen, Mark. *Haunted Indiana.* Holt, MI: Thunder Bay Press (1997).

Slaughter, April. *Ghosthunting Texas (America's Haunted Road Trip).* Cincinnati, OH: Clerisy Press (2009).

Taylor, Troy. *Haunted Alton.* Decatur, IL: Whitechapel Press. (2014).

Read More

Lunis, Natalie. *A Haunted Capital (Scary Places: Cities).* New York: Bearport (2015).

Lunis, Natalie. *Spooky Schools (Scary Places).* New York: Bearport (2013).

Williams, Dinah. *Haunted Houses (Scary Places).* New York: Bearport (2008).

Learn More Online

To learn more about creepy libraries, visit
www.bearportpublishing.com/ScaryPlaces

Index

About the Author

Troy Taylor is the author of more than 110 books on history, hauntings, crime, and the unexplained. He is also the founder of American Hauntings, which offers ghost tours and events all over the country.